D1569276

Stand Up for Trustworthiness

Growing Character

By Frank Murphy

Pioneerland Library System
P.O. Box 327
Willmar, MN 56201

21st Century
Junior Library

Published in the United States of America by
Cherry Lake Publishing
Ann Arbor, Michigan
www.cherrylakepublishing.com

Reading Adviser: Marla Conn, MS, Ed., Literacy specialist, Read-Ability, Inc.

Photo Credits: ©Cat Act Art/Shutterstock, cover, 1; ©Monkey Business Images/Shutterstock, 4; ©Rawpixel.com/Shutterstock, 6; ©Hector Mangharam/Shutterstock, 8; ©SpeedKingz/Shutterstock, 10; ©Rawpixel.com/Shutterstock, 12; ©Tyler Olson/ Shutterstock, 14; ©Twinsterphoto/Shutterstock, 16; ©Val Thoermer/Shutterstock, 18; ©Yuliya Evstratenko/Shutterstock, 20

Copyright © 2020 by Cherry Lake Publishing
All rights reserved. No part of this book may be reproduced or utilized in any
form or by any means without written permission from the publisher.

Library of Congress Cataloging-in-Publication Data

Names: Murphy, Frank, 1966- author.
Title: Stand up for trustworthiness / written by Frank Murphy.
Description: Ann Arbor : Cherry Lake Publishing, 2019. | Series: Growing
    character | Includes bibliographical references and index.
Identifiers: LCCN 2019007445 | ISBN 9781534147430 (hardcover) | ISBN
    9781534148864 (pdf) | ISBN 9781534150294 (pbk.) | ISBN 9781534151727
    (hosted ebook)
Subjects: LCSH: Reliability—Juvenile literature.
Classification: LCC BJ1500.T78 M87 2019 | DDC 179/.9—dc23
LC record available at https://lccn.loc.gov/2019007445

Cherry Lake Publishing would like to acknowledge the work of The Partnership for 21st Century Skills.
Please visit *www.p21.org* for more information.

Printed in the United States of America
Corporate Graphics

CONTENTS

Lexi knew that an adult would be able to figure out who had lost the envelope.

What Is Trustworthiness?

Lexi found an envelope in her school hallway. There was a note written on it that read, "Money for field trip." Lexi knew someone must have dropped it by mistake. She immediately took it to the front office. The principal returned the envelope to the kindergartner who had lost it. The principal thanked Lexi for helping to make their

Because Lexi is trustworthy, the kindergarten class was able to enjoy their field trip together.

school a place where people know they can **trust** one another.

Trust is the **root word** in trustworthiness. When you admit mistakes that you made, show that you are honest, or do what you promised you would do, you are building trust with people. You are becoming trustworthy.

Think!

Think about what would've happened if Lexi had decided to keep the money she found. Think about all the people who would have been affected by her untrustworthy action. Can you think of a time that you were honest?

What chores do your parents trust you to do?

Being Trustworthy

There are many ways to be trustworthy. One way is to be dependable. At home, Lexi does the chores she has told her family she will do. On Sunday nights, she puts the different trash containers out by the street. She makes sure they are in the right place. She doesn't hurry. She does it right! Her family can count on Lexi to do what she promises to do.

Working in a group means that every group member must be trustworthy, fair, and responsible.

Lexi always keeps her promises. She promised her classmates she would help with their group project on Tuesday. After school on Tuesday, Lexi's brother asked her to play basketball. Lexi wanted to play basketball, but she kept her promise to her friends. If you don't keep your word, your friends may not think they can count on you again.

Cheating during a test might help you get a better grade on the test, but it doesn't help you in the long run.

Lexi is also trustworthy when it comes to her learning at school. She never **cheats** on homework or tests. Some people may be **tempted** to look at a classmate's answers on a test. This is not a trustworthy thing to do. Plus using someone else's answers doesn't help your teacher. Your honest answers on tests and homework helps your teacher see how well you are learning. If you

Create!

Make up a story about someone who isn't trustworthy. What might happen to the person? Would he or she learn a lesson about being trustworthy? Tell your story to a parent or a friend when it is done.

The way you treat library books is a good way to show how trustworthy you are.

are having trouble, she will be able to help. Your teachers and classmates should be able to trust your actions.

People who are trustworthy don't take things that do not belong to them. If Lexi sees a backpack on the ground, she doesn't pick it up and go through it looking for things that aren't hers. Instead, she would try to find who the backpack belongs to. A trustworthy person will not steal. Trustworthy people understand that people's belongings should be respected.

When you show your siblings that they can trust you, you are also showing them how to be trustworthy.

Spreading Trust

Your actions can **affect** others in a positive way. If you show that you are trustworthy, other people may decide to do the same. Lexi was in a grocery store with her little brother.

Look!

Pay attention to people who you trust. Look for things they say and do that make them trustworthy. Think about what you can do to be more like them.

See if your family or neighbors need help with yard work or raking leaves.

Lexi saw a man drop his wallet and walk away. The man didn't know he dropped it. Lexi and her little brother could see money sticking out. Lexi picked it up and gave it back to him. Hopefully, Lexi's honesty **inspires** her little brother to do the same thing one day.

Being a trustworthy citizen in your neighborhood is important. Do not take things from your neighbors or businesses. Do not **damage** their property either. Instead, ask people how you can help. Maybe a neighbor needs help with yard work. Maybe a business owner needs help

The more you show you are trustworthy, the more people will trust you.

shoveling snow in front of their building. If you do promise to help, keep your word and follow through with actions. People will notice. This will build trust. And it will show others what being trustworthy looks like.

Being a trustworthy person is a sign to your family, teachers, and neighbors that you are maturing. Trust is a valuable thing. Once it is lost, it is very hard to earn it back. If your actions and words are always honest, you will always be trusted!

GLOSSARY

affect (uh-FEKT) to change someone or something

cheats (CHEETS) acts dishonestly to get the right answer or win a game

damage (DAM-ij) to harm something with the goal of ruining it

inspires (in-SPIREZ) moves someone to act or create something

root word (ROOT WURD) the basic part or origin of a word

tempted (TEMPT-ed) having an urge to do something

trust (TRUHST) belief in the ability of someone to do something

FIND OUT MORE

BOOKS

Small, Mary. *Being Trustworthy: A Book About Trustworthiness.*
Mankato, MN: Picture Window Books, 2006.

Thomas, Pat. *I'm Telling the Truth: A First Look at Honesty.*
Hauppauge, NY: Barron's Educational Series, 2006.

WEBSITE

Stories to Grow By
www.storiestogrowby.com/choose.php
Find stories about keeping promises and other good character traits.

INDEX

ABOUT THE AUTHOR

Frank Murphy has written several books for young readers. They are about famous people, historical events, and leadership. He was born in California but now lives in Pennsylvania with his family.